W9-CCB-277

Winnona Park
Elementary School

ORDINARY PEOPLE CHANGE the WORLD

I am George Washington

BRAD MELTZER

illustrated by Christopher Eliopoulos

DIAL BOOKS FOR YOUNG READERS

I am George Washington.

You know what one of the hardest things in life is?

Being the first.

When you're the first to try something new, there's no one to show you the way.

But when I was little, I wasn't the first. I was the fourth of nine children.

When I was *really* little, I lived at a place called Mount Vernon, which had a huge river running through the backyard and unexplored forests in every direction.

People will tell you that I was a perfect boy.
They'll say I didn't tell a lie after I chopped down a cherry tree.
But that cherry tree story isn't true.
Like most boys back then, I liked swimming . . .
fishing . . .
and riding horses.
I was a decent athlete, but nothing spectacular.
Mostly, I was an ordinary kid.

I liked books, and even liked to dance. I was great at it. In school, my best subject was math. I was pretty good at writing, but I was always a terrible speller.

But remember when I said that it's hard to be the first?
It's easier when there's someone showing you how it's done.

I loved hearing the stories of his adventures.

Thanks to my brother, I knew I wanted to serve in the military.

Soon, though, I saw how uncertain life could be.

When I was eleven, my dad died.

We couldn't afford proper schooling so my brothers had to teach me at home.

I didn't go to high school or college.

But I was committed to learning and building myself.

AS A BOY, I COPIED ALL THE RULES FROM A BOOK OF VIRTUES. THERE WERE 110 IN ALL.
#11: DON'T GNAW YOUR NAILS.
#12: DON'T STAND TOO CLOSE TO PEOPLE WHEN TALKING, OR YOU'LL SPIT ON THEM.
#100: DON'T USE A FORK OR KNIFE TO CLEAN YOUR TEETH. INSTEAD, USE A TOOTHPICK.
THE MOST IMPORTANT WAS THE FIRST ONE.
EVERY ACTION DONE IN COMPANY OUGHT TO BE DONE WITH SOME SIGN OF RESPECT.
I GUESS THAT ONE COVERS SPITTING ON PEOPLE TOO.

When I turned fifteen, my mother told me I needed to get a job.

Since I was good at math and precision, I became a surveyor, someone who explores large areas of land to find their boundaries.

the rain was fierce . . .

and one night, the straw mat I was sleeping on caught fire!
The next night was even harder.

But we kept going.
DON'T GIVE UP!

There was something special in treading a new path, something beautiful in doing what no one had ever done before.

Just being around the Fairfaxes changed my life.
They helped me get work.
I observed how they lived, how they dressed, and how they ate.
I even learned how to properly . . .

At the Fairfaxes',
I ate with fine silver
and beautiful china.

At home, I ate with
sticks at a fire.
It was as if I was
living in two worlds.
But to me, both were
equally important.

When I got older, I joined the military.
In my first big battle, I was on the British side, fighting against the French and Native Americans.
I WAS NEARLY SHOT FOUR TIMES.
FOUR MUSKET BALLS RIPPED THROUGH MY CLOTHING.

We lost the battle, but I became the commander of all of Virginia's fighting forces.

At the age of twenty-three, I ran for office: to be a member of the house of the Virginia legislature.

I lost.

That's right. I lost.

It didn't stop me. I tried again, and this time, I won.

In fact, I won reelection every time after that. But the world as I knew it . . .

was about to change.

Remember, when I was growing up, the United States didn't exist yet.

Back then, there were no states—just colonies, all of them controlled by England.

We were ruled by the British king, named George III.

In April 1775, the first shots were fired in Massachusetts, in Lexington and Concord.

It took eight days for the news of this new "American Revolution" to reach me.

It was one of the biggest questions in history.

The answer came at a meeting called the Second Continental Congress.

Our thirteen colonies decided we would fight together against King George III.

All we needed was a leader for the battle.

Guess who they chose?

Some say it was because I was a natural leader.

Some say it was simply because I was taller than everyone else.

But let me tell you a secret: I was the only one wearing a military uniform.

It wasn't an accident.

On that day, I came ready to lead, ready to do the job, ready to be the first.

Was it easy to be in power?

Never.

Our side didn't have enough food, clothing, or weapons.

Their side was well fed and well armed.

Our side didn't have trained soldiers. We were farmers and fishermen.

Their side was the greatest fighting force in the world.

IN THE WINTER AT VALLEY FORGE, SOME OF OUR TROOPS DIDN'T EAT FOR DAYS.
THEY WORE RAGS AND HAD TO GO BAREFOOT!
IN THE SNOW!

So how'd we win?
We were smarter.
WE WROTE PLANS IN INVISIBLE INK SO THE BRITISH COULDN'T READ THEM. COOL, RIGHT? INVISIBLE INK!
MY CODE NAME WAS 711.
Secret Meeting with 711
We were sneakier.
WE LAUNCHED SURPRISE RAIDS—LIKE THIS ONE, WHERE WE CROSSED THE DELAWARE RIVER.
But most important we wouldn't give in.
THEY WERE FIGHTING FOR A KING.

WE WERE FIGHTING FOR A CAUSE.
FOR FREEDOM!
ALSO, LET'S NOT FORGET: WE HAD A WEAPON THEY'D NEVER HAVE.
WE HAD GENERAL GEORGE WASHINGTON.

After we beat the British army, a new government was formed.

I presided over the convention that wrote our Constitution, which created the new laws for our country.

The brand-new United States of America was free to explore its own future.

Now all we needed was to pick our first president.

Someone brave.

Someone strong.

Someone trustworthy enough to handle all that power.

Again, guess who they chose?

Some say it was my most heroic act.
Instead of putting myself first, I put my faith in my country.
I put my faith in you.

In life, there are many ways to lead.
You can be a quiet leader, a tough leader, a bold leader.
But leadership isn't about being in charge.
It's about taking care of those *in* your charge.

When you're in a position of power, always look out for those who put their faith in you.

And always forge your own road, because sometimes the most important trail is the one no one has ever taken before.

When you do those things, you will clear a path . . .

that will lead the way for others.

FIRST IN WAR, FIRST IN PEACE, AND FIRST IN THE HEARTS OF HIS COUNTRYMEN.
I JUST LIKE THAT HE WORE FAKE TEETH.
THEY WEREN'T MADE OF WOOD, THOUGH. THEY WERE IVORY.
GROSS!
YOU CAN SEE THEM AT MOUNT VERNON.
27

Leadership doesn't come from charisma or personality.
It comes from courage:
The courage to do what's right.
The courage to serve others.
The courage to go first.

I am George Washington.
Today they call me the father of our country.
I have the courage to do what no one's done before.

"I hope I shall always possess . . . virtue enough to maintain . . . the character of an honest man."
—George Washington

Timeline

FEBRUARY 22, 1732 — Born in Westmoreland County, Virginia

APRIL 12, 1743 — Father died

1748 — Joined Lord Fairfax to survey Shenandoah Valley

JULY 1752 — Brother Lawrence died

1754–1763 — French and Indian War

JANUARY 6, 1759 — Married Martha Dandridge Custis

Mount Vernon, George's home

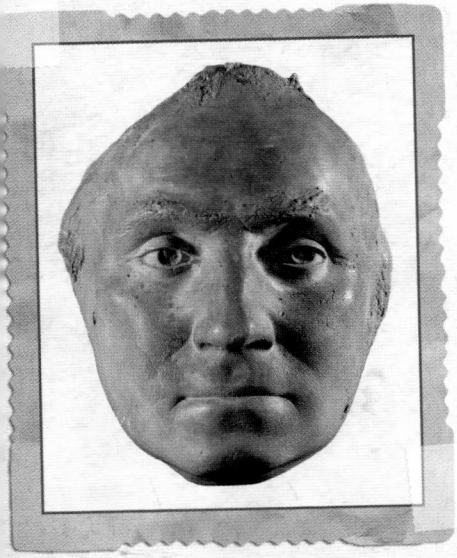

A mask of George's face upon his death

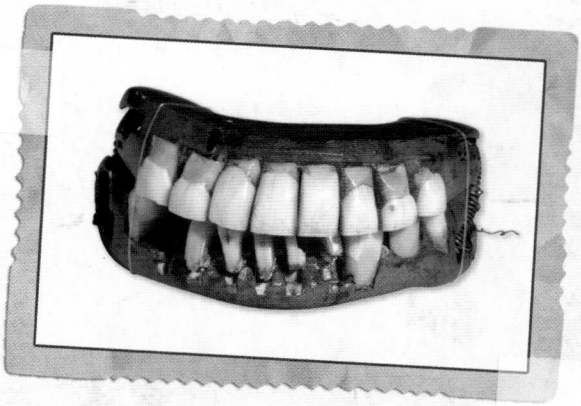

George's fake teeth (gross, right?)

APRIL 1775
attles of Lexington and Concord start merican Revolution

JUNE 15, 1775
Named Commander-in-Chief of Continental Army

DECEMBER 25–26, 1776
Crossed the Delaware River

OCTOBER 19, 1781
British surrender at Yorktown

APRIL 30, 1789
Inaugurated as first U.S. President

DECEMBER 14, 1799
Died at age 67 in Mount Vernon, Virginia

1885
Presidents' Day established

For Eli Segal,
my first boss,
my first real job,
and the first to teach me about
the power of citizen service
and the impact of a great leader.
—B.M.

For Nate Cosby,
who put faith in me,
became my biggest cheerleader,
who pushed me to be a better artist,
but most of all, someone I consider family.
—C.E.

Special thanks to Joseph Ellis for his help and input.
Additional thanks to fearless leader Simon Sinek.

SOURCES

His Excellency: George Washington by Joseph J. Ellis (Vintage Books, 2004)
Washington: A Life by Ron Chernow (Penguin Press, 2010)
Washington: The Indispensable Man by James Thomas Flexner (Back Bay Books, 1994)
George Washington and Benedict Arnold: A Tale of Two Patriots by Dave R. Palmer (Regnery History, 2006)
Founding Father: Rediscovering George Washington by Richard Brookhiser (Free Press, 1996)

FURTHER READING FOR KIDS

Who Was George Washington? by Roberta Edwards (Grosset & Dunlap, 2009)
George Did It by Suzanne Tripp Jurmain (Dutton, 2005)
George Washington's Teeth by Deborah Chandra and Madeleine Comora (Farrar, Straus and Giroux, 2003)
The Founding Fathers!: Those Horse-Ridin', Fiddle-Playin', Book-Readin', Gun-Totin' Gentlemen Who Started America by Jonah Winter (Atheneum, 2015)
Dear Mr. Washington by Lynn Cullen (Dial, 2015)

DIAL BOOKS FOR YOUNG READERS
Penguin Young Readers Group • An imprint of Penguin Random House LLC
375 Hudson Street, New York, NY 10014

Text copyright © 2016 by Forty-four Steps, Inc. • Illustrations copyright © 2016 by Christopher Eliopoulos

Penguin supports copyright. Copyright fuels creativity, encourages diverse voices, promotes free speech, and creates a vibrant culture. Thank you for buying an authorized edition of this book and for complying with copyright laws by not reproducing, scanning, or distributing any part of it in any form without permission. You are supporting writers and allowing Penguin to continue to publish books for every reader.

Library of Congress Cataloging-in-Publication Data
Meltzer, Brad, author.
I am George Washington / Brad Meltzer ; illustrated by Christopher Eliopoulos. • pages cm. — (Ordinary people change the world)
Audience: Ages 5–8. • ISBN 978-0-525-42848-0 (hardcover) • 1. Washington, George, 1732–1799—Juvenile literature. 2. Presidents—United States—Biography—Juvenile literature. 3. Generals—United States—Biography—Juvenile literature. I. Eliopoulos, Chris, illustrator. II. Title. • E312.66.M447 2016 973.4'1092—dc23 [B] 2015036139

Portrait on page 38: Gilbert Stuart (American, 1755–1828), *George Washington*, 1796–1803. Sterling and Francine Clark Art Institute.
Photos on page 39: House and teeth, Courtesy of Mount Vernon Ladies' Association. Death mask, The Pierpont Morgan Library, New York.

Printed in China • 10 9 8 7 6 5 4 3 2 1
Designed by Jason Henry • Text set in Triplex • The artwork for this book was created digitally.